The Little Book of Cooking Together

Simple recipes for young children

Written by
Lorraine Frankish

Edited by Sally Featherstone

Illustrations by Martha Hardy

Little Books with **BIG** ideas®

The Little Book of Cooking Together
ISBN 1 905019 13 0

©Featherstone Education Ltd, 2005
Text ©Lorraine Frankish, 2005
Illustrations ©Martha Hardy, 2005
Series Editor, Sally Featherstone

First published in the UK, March 2005

'Little Books' is a trade mark of Featherstone Education Ltd

The right of Lorraine Frankish to be identified as the author of this work has been asserted in accordance with Sections 77 and 78 of the Copyright, Designs and Patents Act, 1988.

All rights reserved. No part of this publication may be reproduced by any means, stored in a retrieval system, or transmitted in any form or by any means, electronic, mechanical, photocopying, recording or otherwise, without the prior written consent of the publisher. This book may not be lent, sold, hired out or otherwise disposed of by way of trade in any form of binding or with any cover other than that in which it is published without the prior consent of the publisher, and without this condition being imposed upon the subsequent user.

Published in the United Kingdom by
Featherstone Education Ltd
44 - 46 High Street
Husbands Bosworth
Leicestershire
LE17 6LP

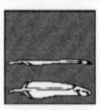

Printed in the UK on paper produced in the European Union from managed, sustainable forests

Contents

Focus of the page	page number
Introduction	4 and 5
Links with the Early Learning Goals	6
Getting Started	7
Hygiene and developing healthy eating habits	8
Health, Safety and Cultural Sensitivity	9
Measurements and Conversion tables	10 and 11
Icing Biscuits	12 and 13
Muesli	14 and 15
DIY Salad	16 and 17
Sandwiches	18 and 19
All Toasty	20 and 21
Fill a Pitta Pocket or Two	22 and 23
Saucy Tomatoes	24 and 25
Quick Pizza	26 and 27
Choppers' Vegetable Soup	28 and 29
Bake a Loaf	30 and 31
Garlic Bread	32 and 33
Pat a Chapatti	34 and 35
Vegetable Curry	36 and 37
A Taste of the Middle East	38 and 39
Potato Cakes	40 and 41
Fruit Kebabs	42 and 43
Pile it High	44 and 45
Banana Custard	46 and 47
Toss a Pancake	48 and 49
Baked Apples	50 and 51
Choc Chip Muffins	52 and 53
Make a Teddy Face	54 and 55
Jam Tarts	56 and 57
Banana Fudge for Divali	58 and 59
Hot Chocolate	60 and 61
Milk Shakes and Smoothies	62 and 63
Fruit Punch	64 and 65
Tea Tasters Time	66 and 67

The Little Book of Cooking Together

Introduction

Cooking is a life skill that all children should have the opportunity to learn and the Foundation Stage is a good time to start developing it. Of course, some children will come to your setting already experienced in food preparation and cooking, but others will have little experience of how the food they eat arrives on the plate. Convenience foods and microwave ovens speed up the processes, and we can use these in settings when a more instant result is desirable!

The Little Book of Cooking Together gives you a range of simple recipes which encourage children to work independently except for the hot or risky stages, ensuring the children will gain practical experience while having fun and enjoyment.

The Foundation Stage Guidance

The Guidance for the Foundation Stage Curriculum states that practitioners should:

* plan for the development of independence skills;
* demonstrate the use of language for reading and writing;
* ensure children enjoy mathematical learning because it is purposeful;
* plan a range of mathematical opportunities;
* give opportunities (some may be adult directed) to investigate using a range of techniques and senses;
* teach children how to use tools effectively and safely;
* provide opportunities for children to practice and refine their skills.

Cooking is a great way to cover these elements of the Foundation Stage curriculum in enjoyable and practical ways. Through appropriate activities, and sensitive questioning during these activities children can increase their experience by:

* using scientific processes in Knowledge and Understanding of the World, as they see first hand the effect of heat, mixing, colouring and diluting on solids and liquids;
* learning the importance in Mathematical Development of measuring accurately using scales and other equipment;
* using tools and equipment, essential for Technological Development;
* following instructions and recipes which contribute to Communication and Language Development;
* trying new flavours and textures, using their senses to explore materials and foods, and creating food to enjoy and share. These are all part of Creative Development;
* understanding other's cultures and beliefs, developing likes and dislikes, working independently, and working with others - all contributing to Personal and Social Development;

and finally, all cooking activities give children opportunities to practice the fine motor control essential for their Physical Development.

The Little Book of Cooking Together

Links with the Early Learning Goals

You will find individual stepping stones and goals on each activity page. Some of the key goals for cooking are listed here:

Personal, Social and Emotional Development
- form good relationships with adults and peers;
- work as part of a group, taking turns and sharing fairly;
- understand that people have different needs, views, cultures and beliefs that need to be treated with respect;
- have a developing awareness of their own needs, views and feelings and be sensitive to the needs, views and feelings of others;
- select and use resources independently.

Communication, language and literacy
- interact with others, negotiating plans and activities and taking turns in conversation;
- extend their vocabulary, exploring the meanings and sounds of new words;
- use talk to organise, sequence and clarify thinking, ideas feelings & events.

Mathematical Development
- use language such as lighter and heavier to compare quantities;
- say and use number names in order.

Knowledge and Understanding of the World
- investigate objects and materials by using all of their senses;
- select tools and techniques they need to shape, assemble and join the materials they are using;
- look closely at similarities, differences, patterns and change;
- find out about and identify the uses of everyday technology;
- know about their own cultures and beliefs and those of other people.

Physical Development
- move with confidence, imagination and in safety;
- recognise the importance of keeping healthy and those things which contribute to this;
- use a range of small and large equipment;
- handle tools, objects, construction and malleable materials safely and with increasing control.

Creative Development
- respond to what they see, hear, smell, touch and feel;
- express their ideas through designing and making.

Getting Started

Planning and preparation

To gain the most from each recipe, aim to involve the children fully whenever possible. Get them to contribute to the whole process, including planning and shopping. This will involve working in small groups with good adult support. Small group work supports good learning!

Cooking facilities in early years settings will vary and with this in mind the suggested recipes are simple. Many do not require a cooker, however if you do not have access to a cooker it may be worth investing in either a single electric hot ring that will not take up too much storage space, or a simple microwave oven.

Equipment and ingredients

The equipment and ingredients recommended are easily available at a reasonable cost. Remember to keep equipment separate from other resources and ensure that it is used solely for cooking activities. Once you have chosen a recipe, check that you have the equipment you will need, and make sure that there will be enough to avoid children having to wait for any undue length of time.

Unless stated, each recipe is for a group of four children. As in all recipes, results can vary depending on humidity, amount of handling and the type of cooker used. So try the recipe out first before attempting it with the children.

Hygiene

Ingredients should be stored hygienically and at the correct temperature. A cool box with ice packs can be used if food is not going to be stored overnight. Children should be encouraged to get into the routine of washing their hands before handling food and wearing a clean apron – one that is kept exclusively for cooking. Allow plenty of time, so that children do not feel hurried. They will be picking up many skills that will help them in other areas of their development. Planning time for clearing away can also provide valuable learning. Although cooking with young children usually involves a certain amount of mess, clearing away and washing the table can be made into a fun and worthwhile activity.

Trying something new

Eating together is an excellent social activity, but it should not be viewed as the ultimate goal. Sometimes children will try something that they would not normally eat because they have prepared it themselves or because they are with their friends. Growing your own ingredients is another good way of encouraging children to try new flavours and recipes. However, do not be disappointed if some of the children decide that they do not like what they have cooked. This is all part of the learning process.

Health, Safety and Cultural Sensitivity

Before starting any of the recipes it is vital that you are fully aware of any children who have special diets for health, cultural or religious reasons.

> Some children may also have allergic reactions to particular foods. You MUST check each time you cook that the ingredients are safe for the whole group. Remember that a trace of something on a spoon or bowl is sometimes enough to trigger an allergic reaction. Keep up-to-date records and adapt or choose recipes accordingly.

There is an element of risk involved in cooking activities, as children will be working with knives (blunt knives are harder to work with and actually can be more of a risk), electrical equipment or occasional spills on the floor. However with careful management this should not be a problem. Always make sure there is adequate adult supervision when children are using kitchen equipment. Store dangerous equipment out of reach of children.

Teach them basic safety rules:

- * ovens and pans can be hot and if touched may burn;
- * never start cooking without an adult present;
- * knives are sharp and should be handled carefully;
- * the resources are real, not toys, and children must use them with care;
- * sleeves should be rolled up, long hair tied back;
- * fingers and hands need to be clean to keep everyone healthy.

Adult instructions or stages are printed in red in each recipe.

Conversion tables

The recipes in this book are in a mixture of measurement types. Some are in cups, some in spoons, some in metric measures. It is important for children to realise early that measurements come in a range of types.

Here are conversion tables so you know how to convert a recipe if you don't have the right measuring utensils.

NB don't mix different sorts of measures in the same recipe!!

Cups and Millilitres
(use the same cup each time!)

1 cup	250ml
half a cup	125ml
third of a cup	80ml
quarter of a cup	60ml

Spoons & Millilitres

1 tablespoon	15ml
1 teaspoon	5ml
half a teaspoon	2.5ml
quarter teaspoon	1.25ml

Ounces and grams

Ounces	grams
1oz	28g
2oz	57g
3oz	85g
4oz	114g
5oz	142g
6oz	170g
7oz	175g
8oz	203g
9oz	227g
10oz	255g
16oz/1lb	454g
2lb	907g

Level tablespoons in grams

1 tablespoon rice	15g
1 tablespoon sugar	15g
1 tablespoon butter/margarine	15g
1 tablespoon flour (not sifted)	8g
1 tablespoon Parmesan cheese	5g
1 tablespoon breadcrumbs	3-4g

Fluid Ounces and tablespoons

8 fluid ounces	16 tablespoons
4 fluid ounces	8 tablespoons
3 fluid ounces	5 tablespoons
2 fluid ounces	4 tablespoons

Cups and grams

1 cup of sugar	200g
1 cup of sifted flour	115g
1 cup of flour spooned from bag	120g/4 oz
1 cup of flour dredged from the bag	140g

Oven temperatures

Gas mark	Centigrade	Fahrenheit
1/4	110°	225°F
1/2	130°C	250°F
1	140°C	275°F
2	150°C	300°F
3	160°C	325°F
4	180°C	350°F
5	190°C	375°F
6	200°C	400°F
7	220°C	425°F
8	230°C	450°F

Icing Biscuits

A simple activity and a good one to help with fine motor skills as well as creativity. It is quick to prepare and uses simple resources, providing a useful introduction to cookery.

What you need:

- plain biscuits, such as Rich Tea or Osborne
- 100g icing sugar
- 1 tablespoon warm water
- a few drops of food colouring (optional)
- an assortment of cake decorations; hundreds and thousands, dried fruit, chocolate sprinkles, coconut
- dessert or butter knives
- straws, scales, sieves, small bowls, jugs, aprons

Links with the Early Learning Goals

PSED be confident to try new activities, initiate ideas & speak in a familiar group;

KUW investigate objects & materials by using all of their senses;

KUW ask questions about why things happen and how things work;

PD handle tools, objects, construction & malleable materials safely and with increasing control.

What you do:

Children can ice biscuits independently. They may need help with making icing the first time they do it.

1. Help them to weigh or measure the icing sugar and sift it into a bowl. Look at the icing sugar dust as it moves in the air. Can they smell and taste it?
2. Gradually add water a little at a time until the icing is soft and firm.
3. For coloured icing, suggest they could add a few drops of food colouring and mix until the colour is even.
4. Watch and talk about the changes as the colouring is absorbed and becomes even.
5. Spoon the icing over the biscuits and smooth with a dessert knife. Children can add spots, dots or lines of different colours, drizzling the icing from a spoon or a straw.
6. Do several biscuits each, then the first ones can dry a bit ready for decorating (if you put decorations on too soon, they may slide off again or their colour may run).
7. Add toppings of choice. As you all work, talk about textures, colours and shapes. Don't forget to use all your senses!
8. Eat and enjoy!

And another idea . . .

* Flavour the icing with cocoa powder, a few drops of vanilla essence or just a drop of peppermint oil.
* Spread tomato paste or cream cheese on savoury or cheese biscuits. Decorate with grated cheese, sliced gherkins or chopped peppers and tomatoes.
* Cheese in a tube is fun!

Muesli

Muesli ingredients can vary according to taste, so children will need to make choices and think about quantities. It is usually made and left to soak overnight but can be eaten immediately.

What you need:
- 1 tablespoon rolled oats
- 1 tbsp wheat flakes
- 1 tbsp barley flakes
- 1 tbsp dried fruit - sultanas or raisins
- 1 tablespoon chopped nuts such as hazelnuts (optional)
- 6 tablespoons water or milk
- cereal bowl and spoon
- tablespoons and teaspoons
- small bowls for ingredients

Check for cereal, nut or dairy sensitivity before embarking on this activity.

Links with the Early Learning Goals

PSED select and use activities and resources independently;

MA in practical activities & discussion begin to use the vocabulary involved in adding & subtracting;

CD respond to what they see, hear, smell, touch and feel;

PD handle tools, & malleable materials safely and with increasing control.

What you do:

Shopping for the ingredients is a good preparation for all cooking activities. Use a shopping trip to look at different sorts of cereal.

1. The children can help to tip the dry ingredients into separate bowls.
2. Look closely at each of the ingredients together and talk about the differences.
3. Invite the children to choose what to include and add to their cereal bowl a spoonful at a time.
4. Show them how to mix all the ingredients together. Watch what happens.
5. Add the milk a bit at a time and watch again. If you leave the mixture for a few minutes it will begin to thicken. Talk about the mixture as it thickens. Add more milk until it is the desired consistency.
6. Sit somewhere comfortable, indoors or out, to eat your muesli.
7. The birds will eat any leftovers!

And another idea . . .

* Try offering chopped fresh fruit to add to the muesli - you could try apple, orange, pear, strawberries or blueberries.
* Dried apricots, berries and banana are good for variety and they all contribute to healthy eating.
* Look in a health food shop for different sorts of grains to add.

The Little Book of Cooking Together

DIY Salad

Any salad ingredients can be used, but variety will make the salad more interesting. Avocado is an interesting addition, easy to prepare and soft to eat.

What you need:
- 1 cucumber
- 250g tomatoes
- 1 carrot
- lettuce or other salad leaves
- 150ml vegetable oil
- 70ml lemon juice
- 1 avocado
- vegetable knife
- chopping board
- salad bowl
- a lidded beaker or plastic bottle
- salad servers

Links with the Early Learning Goals

PSED be confident to try new activities, initiate ideas & speak in a familiar group;

CLL extend their vocabulary, exploring meanings & sounds of new words;

KUW look closely at similarities, differences, patterns & change; investigate objects & materials by using all of their senses;

PD handle tools safely & with control.

What you do:

1. Wash the salad ingredients well and look closely at and feel each piece. Name the ingredients together and talk about the smell, colour, size, texture (such as ridges on the cucumber), weight and shape.
2. Look carefully at the avocado. Feel and smell it before you wipe the skin. Talk about why it's called an avocado **pear**.
3. Help the children to slice the cucumber and cut the tomatoes in half on the chopping board.
4. They can also peel or scrub the carrot and carefully grate it or cut it into small pieces.
5. Tear the lettuce or other leaves into pieces.
6. Cut the avocado in half and remove the stone, and let the children cut it into slices.
7. Arrange all the ingredients into a salad bowl.
8. Put the salad dressing ingredients (the oil and lemon juice) into a lidded beaker or screw topped jar.
9. Make sure the lid is secure before taking turns to shake it well.
10. Pour a few drops over the salad just before eating, and toss the salad gently with salad servers.

And another idea . . .

* Use a salad spinner to dry the lettuce - children love these!
* Add some other ingredients such as grated cheese, raisins, grapes, grated beetroot, chopped celery or apple, home made croutons.
* Plant the avocado stone in a pot of compost and put it in a warm place to grow.

Sandwiches

The choice of fillings for sandwiches is endless, and the simple activity helps with fine motor skills and independent learning. Visit a baker for different kinds of bread to extend the choices.

What you need for 4 children:
- 8 slices of bread
- soft margarine or butter
- chopping board or clean work surface
- dessert knives
- bowls and spoons for fillings
- filling of choice: younger children could start with easy fillings such as sliced cucumber, Marmite, cheese spread or jam. Older children will be able to manage chopped hard boiled egg, grated cheese etc

Links with the Early Learning Goals

PSED select & use activities & resources independently;

KUW select the tools and techniques they need to shape, assemble & join the materials they are using;

PD handle tools, objects, construction & malleable materials safely and with increasing control.

What you do:

1. Look at the bread together and share new words to describe how it smells, feels, looks. Introduce words such as crust, crumbs, slice.
2. Give each child two slices of bread.
3. If they need it, show them how to use the knife to spread the butter/margarine over both slices of bread.
4. Encourage them to work carefully to cover the whole area. Some children become VERY absorbed in this - give them time, it may be their first independent experience.
5. Help them to cover one slice with the filling, place the second slice on top and <u>gently</u> press down.
6. Most children will be able to cut their sandwich by themselves. Talk about the shapes they can make by cutting them in different ways. Use half and quarter, square and triangle.
7. Arrange the sandwich on a plate before eating!
8. This snack is an easy way to encourage independence and choice without overwhelming children with a difficult task. You could provide ready cut half or quarter slices as well as whole ones to cater for smaller appetites.

And another idea . . .

* Use cutters to cut the sandwiches into animal or other shapes. You could also try cutting a shape in the top slice to reveal the filling!
* Make sandwiches for a party or special event.
* Try a variety of different breads: wholemeal, sliced and unsliced, granary, rye, seeded.

The Little Book of Cooking Together

All Toasty

Making toast is a very popular activity. It obviously needs some supervision as children should not use a toaster on their own. But the rest of the process is another totally independent activity.

What you need for 4 children:
- 4 (or more) slices of bread
- soft butter or margarine
- a choice of spreads and jams
- toaster
- dessert knives
- plates

Links with the Early Learning Goals

CLL use language to imagine & recreate roles & experiences;

KUW look closely at similarities, differences, patterns & change; ask questions about why things happen and how things work; find out about & identify the uses of everyday technology;

PD handle tools, safely and with increasing control.

What you do:

Use this activity as an opportunity to talk about safe behaviour near hot things. Make sure the toaster is in a safe place and supervised at all times.

1. Look at the bread before it has been toasted. Talk about how the toaster works, and emphasise safe use.
2. Talk about the different settings on the toaster, from light, medium to dark and turn the dial to one of the settings.
3. **Put one slice of bread in the toaster, switch it on.** Watch the bread disappear into the toaster as you press the lever down. Talk about what they think is happening inside the toaster and how it knows the toast is cooked.
4. Sing a toast song such as this while you wait for the toast to cook:
   One square bread slice, turning into toast,
   One square bread slice, turning into toast,
   One square bread slice, turning into toast
   Hurry up toaster, I'm waiting for my toast! (10 Green Bottles tune)
5. Listen for the toast to pop up, **remove it from the toaster and put it on a plate.** Look at what has happened to the bread, and when cool, feel its texture.
6. Help the children, if they need it, to use a knife to cover the toast with butter or margarine.
7. **Toast more bread as you need it.**

And another idea . . .

* Toast a variety of shaped slices from round, bloomer or farmhouse loaves. Talk about the shape and size of the slices and how they fit the toaster.
* Make a dance or movement sequence. Crouch down together and when someone calls 'Toast ready', all jump up.

The Little Book of Cooking Together

Fill a Pitta Pocket or Two

Pitta is a traditional bread of Greece and the Middle East, and is readily available in supermarkets. Crunchy fillings make a nice contrast to the softness of the pitta bread pocket.

What you need for 4 children:

- 4 small pitta bread pockets
- 2 medium carrots, grated
- 2 tomatoes
- 4 lettuce leaves
- 1/2 cup of grated cheese
- mayonnaise or salad cream
- aprons
- chopping boards
- vegetable knives
- mixing bowls

Links with the Early Learning Goals

CLL extend their vocabulary, exploring the meanings & sounds of new words;

CD respond in a variety of ways to what they see, hear, smell, touch and feel;

PD handle tools, objects, construction & malleable materials safely and with increasing control.

What you do:
1. Wash the lettuce and put the leaves on the chopping board and cut into shreds. Younger children can tear the leaves.
2. Grate the cheese and carrot. Slice the tomatoes.
3. Place the tomatoes and shredded lettuce in a bowl with the grated carrots and cheese.
4. Mix everything together gently.
   n.b. The pittas will be much tastier if you can warm them for just a few seconds in a microwave.
5. Cut a 10cm slit along the side of each pitta.
6. Help the children to fill each pocket with the salad.

And another idea . . .
* Use pitta bread as a quick base for pizzas (see page 26 for suggested toppings).
* Try tortilla wraps instead of pitta.
* Draw up a list together of suggested fillings. You don't have to try all of them, but it will encourage children to be imaginative about ingredients.

Saucy Tomatoes

This is a tasty sauce and there are many things to put with it. Try it on wholemeal toast or in the middle of a baguette, sprinkled with a little cheese and heated under a grill or oven.

What you need:

- 1 onion finely chopped
- 1 clove of garlic
- 1 can of chopped tomatoes
- tablespoon olive oil
- pinch of dried basil
- 1 bay leaf
- can opener
- vegetable knife
- chopping board
- garlic press
- saucepan, wooden spoon
- hand held blender (optional)

Links with the Early Learning Goals

PSED be confident to try new activities, initiate ideas & speak in a familiar group;

KUW investigate objects & materials by using all of their senses;

PD handle tools, objects, construction & malleable materials safely and with increasing control.

What you do:

1. Take opportunities when using packets and tins to look together at some of the writing, logos, numbers etc. It's also interesting to look at and read the list of ingredients.
2. Talk about using herbs for flavour and examine the dried basil and bay leaf. Look at a whole onion and then see what it looks like when chopped.
3. Look at the garlic press and talk about how it works. Peel one clove and work with the children to squeeze the clove with the garlic press.
4. Heat the oil in the saucepan and cook the garlic and onions until soft and transparent. You can show the children what is happening, but be careful of the hot pan!
5. Open the can of tomatoes and let the children tip them into a bowl so they can look at them. Add the tomatoes and herbs to the onion mixture and heat through.
6. For a smoother sauce, place the blender into the pan. Make sure it is touching the bottom and remains there while you are blending. Switch on and blend until smooth, and remember to switch it off before removing from the sauce.
7. Encourage the children to talk about the smells!
8. Place on toast, in a baguette or over cooked pasta.

And another idea . .

And another idea . . ..
* Try tomatoes in different ways: fresh, pureed, ketchup, juice.
* Grow tomatoes in a grow bag.
* Look at a variety of edible leaves together. Try lettuce, cabbage, spinach, and other herbs. Remind the children that not all leaves are edible.

Quick Pizza

Pizza is a favourite food, and can be made in a variety of ways. This basic bread base covered with tomato sauce and sprinkled with cheese will produce a snack which most children will love.

What you need for 4 children:
- 2 large round bread baps, rolls or burger buns
- 1 portion of tomato sauce (see recipe on previous page)
- 55g of grated cheese (mozzarella is traditional but any mild cheese will do just as well)
- chopping board or clean work surface
- bread knife
- tablespoon, teaspoon
- baking tray
- access to an oven or grill

Links with the Early Learning Goals

PSED be confident to try new activities;
KUW investigate objects & materials by using all of their senses; find out about & identify the uses of everyday technology;
PD handle tools, objects, construction & malleable materials safely and with increasing control.

What you do:

1. Before you start, look together at the rolls or buns. Talk about how they feel and smell.
2. Put the rolls etc on the board or worktop and help the children to slice each one in two to make two bases for the pizzas.
3. Heat the grill or oven (230C/450/Gas mark 8). Warn the children about hot surfaces, and if possible keep them well away.
4. Now, using the tablespoon, the children can place a spoonful of tomato sauce in the centre of the bap.
5. Help them to spread the sauce across the surface of the bread, using a teaspoon. Encourage them to make sure the children cover the bread right to the edges.
6. Sprinkle grated cheese on top of the sauce.
7. The children can lift the pizzas carefully onto the baking tray.
8. Cook on the top shelf of the oven or under the grill for about 10 minutes until the cheese is melted. Allow to cool before the children handle them.
9. When they are cool enough, each child can cut their own in any way they wish before eating or sharing them with friends.

And another idea . . .

* Buy fresh, growing basil (from a supermarket) and let the children use their senses to investigate it. Add a few leaves to your pizzas after cooking.
* Use the bread recipe on page 30 to make pizza bases.
* Turn your role play area into a pizza parlour, with take-aways and menus.

Choppers' Vegetable Soup

Another great activity for developing hand control, soup is easy to make and delicious to eat. It is also very economical, as the ingredients can be adjusted according to the season.

What you need:

- 225g root vegetables (carrots, potatoes, parsnips, swede etc) use more if you want enough for the whole group
- 1 large onion
- 25g butter or margarine
- 600ml water
- chopping boards
- knives suitable for the children to use
- saucepan, jug
- wooden spoons

Links with the Early Learning Goals

PSED work as part of a group or class, taking turns & sharing fairly;

CLL extend their vocabulary, exploring the meanings & sounds of new words;

KUW investigate objects & materials by using all of their senses; find out about, and identify some features of, living things, objects and events they observe.

What you do:

1. Talk about the ingredients, sorting them and using all your senses to explore them. Some children may not recognise the vegetables in their raw state. Name them and use descriptive words for the way they look, smell, feel.
2. Show the children the recipe in this book, and read what the instructions say.
3. Put the ingredients in the order that they will be required and talk about the recipe. Introduce and explain words that may be new, such as bite-size, sauté and simmer. Although it is essential that an adult takes over when the ingredients are being heated, children can do most of the preparation and watch at a safe distance as the soup is cooked.
4. Peel the vegetables and wash thoroughly.
5. Chop all the vegetables into bite-size pieces on the chopping board. Help them if they need it.
6. Melt the butter in the saucepan, add the vegetables and stir.
7. Sauté the vegetables for a few minutes, stirring all the time.
8. Pour in the water and bring to the boil.
9. Reduce the heat and simmer for 20 minutes until the vegetables are cooked. Encourage talk about the smells!

And another idea . . .

* Hide some root vegetables in a large tray of compost or sand for the children to discover and hide again.
* Look at packaging together and try some other soups, such as canned, condensed, dried, or in cartons.
* Grow your own vegetables in grow bags or your garden. It's worth the wait!

The Little Book of Cooking Together

Bake a Loaf

The beauty of making bread is that it is not spoiled by enthusiastic handling! This recipe is fairly quick to make. Fresh yeast is available at supermarkets, but you can use dried yeast instead.

What you need for 4 children:
- 200g plain flour
- 25g solid vegetable fat
- 15g fresh yeast
- 1 teaspoon lemon juice
- 140ml warmed milk or water
- 1/2 teaspoon salt
- 1/2 teaspoon castor sugar
- scales, measuring spoons, measuring jug, sieve
- baking tray, mixing bowl, small bowls, plastic bags or cling film
- microwave (quicker, but not essential)
- conventional oven

Links with the Early Learning Goals

KUW look closely at similarities, differences, patterns & change; ask questions about why things happen and how things work;

PD handle tools, objects, construction & malleable materials safely and with increasing control;

CD explore colour, texture, shape, form and space in two and three dimensions.

What you do:

At each stage talk about the changes taking place and encourage the children to use their senses: looking, smelling, feeling, tasting, even listening.

1. Heat the oven to 400F/200°C/Gas mark 6.
2. Sieve the flour into the bowl and show the children how to rub in the fat and salt until it resembles fine breadcrumbs.
3. Let the children cream the yeast and sugar together in a small bowl. When this turns liquid, let them add the lemon juice.
4. Warm the milk (or milk and water) a little in the microwave, and help the children to stir a little of this into their flour mixture.
5. Now add the yeast mixture with enough of the remaining milk mixture to make a soft but not too sticky dough.
6. Place the dough in the microwave for 30 seconds on full power (or in a warm place for half an hour) to prove. Remove and knead thoroughly on a floured surface.
7. Divide the dough into 4 pieces so that each child can shape a round ball. Put these on a greased baking tray in a warm place or wrap the tray in a plastic bag for two or three minutes.
8. Bake in a hot oven for 8 to 10 minutes until risen well and golden brown.
9. Allow to cool and spread with butter, jam, honey or cheese!

And another idea . . .

* The dough can be made up to the final stage and then formed into a variety of shapes - animals, faces or figures.
* Make 'cottage rolls' with a larger and a smaller ball of dough. Put the smaller one on top of the larger and push a finger through both balls to fix them together.

Garlic Bread

This recipe can be made in stages if required, as the garlic spread can be prepared at before, and kept tightly covered in a refrigerator. The finished bread could be wrapped in foil for children to take home.

What you need for 4 children:
- 4 long crusty bread rolls or small French sticks
- 2 gloves of garlic
- 80g soft butter or margarine
- dried or fresh parsley
- chopping board, scissors
- bread knife
- small knife
- garlic press
- small bowl
- teaspoon
- foil

Links with the Early Learning Goals

MD Use language such as 'more' or 'less', 'greater' or 'smaller', 'heavier' or 'lighter', to compare two numbers or quantities;

KUW look closely at similarities, differences, patterns & change; find out about & identify the uses of everyday technology;

PD handle tools, objects, construction & malleable materials safely.

What you do:

1. Talk about the colour and texture of the butter and look at it again after it has been heated and melted.
2. Examine the garlic bulb together and pull out individual garlic cloves. Feel the papery texture of the outside of the garlic and compare it with the smoothness of the clove once this is removed.
3. Heat the oven to 200C°/400F/Gas Mark 6.
4. Put the bread on the chopping board and slice in half lengthwise. The children could do this with help.
5. Place the peeled garlic clove into the press and help the children squeeze the handles together to mince the garlic.
6. Put the minced garlic and butter into a small bowl and mix together.
7. If you are using fresh parsley, the children can chop it with scissors in a small mug. Add the parsley and mix.
8. Spread the garlic butter on one side of the rolls or bread, adding more as required until the surface is thickly covered.
9. Wrap in a piece of foil.
10. Bake for about 15 minutes until the butter has melted.
    NB If you have no oven, send the bread home after point 9.

And another idea . . .

* Change the flavour of the butter by introducing different herbs, such as rosemary, thyme, oregano or basil.
* Add a garlic press to playdough resources (not the same one as you cook with though!). Children will love making 'worms', 'spaghetti' or hair.

The Little Book of Cooking Together

Pat a Chapatti

This basic Asian recipe produces a plain unleavened 'fried' bread that is popular with children. They will enjoy patting it from one hand to another to prepare it for the pan.

What you need for each child:
- 4 tablespoons of wholemeal flour
- a pinch of salt
- warm water

you also need:
- measuring spoons
- measuring jugs, sieves
- mixing bowls
- rolling pin
- hot ring
- frying pan
- spatula

Links with the Early Learning Goals

PSED select and use activities & resources independently;
KUW investigate objects & materials by using all of their senses; begin to know about their own cultures & beliefs & those of other people;
PD handle tools, objects, construction & malleable materials safely and with increasing control.

What you do:

1. Talk with the children about the different kinds of bread they have tried and tell them that this is a flat bread that is often eaten with curry.
2. Help the children to measure the flour, sieve it into the bowl and mix in the water to make a soft dough.
3. Turn out on to a floured board or table and knead thoroughly.
4. Using rolling pins, roll out thinly.
5. Pick up the flattened dough and pat from one hand to another. The chapatti will increase in size and get thinner as you pat.
6. Heat the pan and cook each chapatti quickly (you do not need to grease the pan).
7. Cook until it is beginning to singe and puffs up, turning once during cooking.
8. Eat as they are or with curry (see page 36/37), or plain yogurt mixed with chopped cucumber and lemon juice.

And another idea . . .

* Make chapattis outside and have a chapatti picnic.
* Give the children simple chapatti dough to play with, without cooking.
* Sing:
  One chapatti, two chapatti,
  Three chapatti, four,
  Five chapatti, six chapatti,
  Let's all make some more!
  (to the One Potato, Two Potato Rhythm).

Vegetable Curry

This is a basic, but tasty curry. As chilli and other hot spices are not used it is mild in flavour. The spices are available in supermarkets, and you can use a combination of whatever vegetables are available.

What you need:
- 1 tablespoon of vegetable oil
- 1/2 teaspoon cumin seeds
- 1/2 teaspoon mustard seeds
- 1 teaspoon garam masala
- 1/2 teaspoon coriander
- 1/2 teaspoon ground cumin
- 2 tablespoons water
- approximately 225g of vegetables – try broccoli, potatoes, carrots, tomatoes, even some frozen peas
- saucepan with a lid
- teaspoons, tablespoon

Links with the Early Learning Goals

PSED have a developing respect for their own cultures and beliefs and those of other people;

CLL sustain attentive listening, responding to what they have heard by relevant comments, questions or actions;

CD respond in a variety of ways to what they see, hear, smell, touch and feel.

What you do:

This dish can be eaten alone, but also goes well with chapatti (previous recipe) or plain boiled rice, which you could microwave.

1. Take time to examine the vegetables before you wash and peel them. Compare the look, feel and smell of them before and after. Encourage the use of new words to describe textures and smells.
2. Together, chop the vegetables into small chunks. Younger or less dextrous children can get involved in preparing vegetables by scrubbing carrots and washing broccoli.
3. Now look at the spices. Smell them and feel the whole seeds in your fingers. Talk about where spices grow.
4. Heat the oil in the pan and add the cumin and mustard seeds.
5. Cover the pan and listen to the seeds 'pop'. Remove when the seeds no longer pop and let the oil cool. Have a look at the seeds now.
6. Add the vegetables and water to the pan.
7. Sprinkle in the remaining spices.
8. Cover tightly and simmer slowly for about 20 minutes.
9. Stir frequently, adding water if required to prevent sticking.

And another idea . . .

* Try grinding whole spices in a mortar and pestle so the children can see how they change from seed to powder.
* Set up a sensory table and introduce a range of spices for children to smell and talk about. Include cumin, coriander, cardamom, nutmeg, ginger, cinnamon and paprika.
* Make smelly pictures by painting glue on black paper and sprinkling with spices.

The Little Book of Cooking Together

A Taste of The Middle East

Couscous can be eaten warm or cold, as a sweet or savoury dish, and for some children it may be a new taste or texture. Once children have learned how to make it they can add other ingredients to make it even tastier.

What you need for 4 children:
- 150g of couscous
- a little salt
- 250ml of boiling water
- 2 tablespoons of vegetable oil
- scales
- bowls
- forks
- teaspoon
- tablespoon
- measuring jug
- kitchen timer
- clingfilm
- flavourings (see recipe point 9)

Links with the Early Learning Goals

PSED be confident to try new activities, initiate ideas & speak in a familiar group; select and use activities and resources independently;

KUW investigate objects & materials by using all of their senses; ask questions about why things happen and how things work.

What you do:

1. Talk to the children about the recipe and what you are about to do.
2. Look at the couscous packet and tip a bit of dry couscous out for them to explore with their fingers.
3. Measure the couscous into a bowl that allows for swelling.
4. Mix in the salt.
5. Explain that couscous needs very hot water, and they must stay safely away from the kettle. Make sure they sit down during this part. Boil the kettle and pour the boiling water into the measuring jug. Then pour the water into the bowl with the couscous. It is essential that an adult pours the boiling water well away from the children.
6. Fork the water through to break up the grains. Add the oil. Cover the bowl with cling film so the children can still see it.
7. Once you have done this bit, children can work independently. Talk about how the grains change when water is added, and use a timer so that the children can measure the 10 minutes.
8. Remove the cling film and give them a fork to break down any grains that have stuck together - they could do it with (clean) fingers.
9. Add any of the following: thinly sliced fried onions, chopped peppers or tomatoes, sultanas, banana or other diced fruit.
10. Couscous makes a great snack, as you can make it sweet or savoury and different every time.

And another idea . . .

* Dried couscous can be used to make great sound shakers. Put a handful of couscous grains in small plastic bottles (bio yogurt drink bottles are an ideal size for a child's hand). Seal them and let the children decorate them to play at music time.

Potato Cakes

Potato cakes (also called latkes) are cheap and easy to make. They are also delicious. This recipe does involve two stages of simple cooking, with necessary safety implications!

What you need:
- 4 medium potatoes (or more for a bigger group)
- half a teaspoon of salt
- 6 tablespoons of milk
- 6 tablespoons of grated cheese
- a little flour for dusting
- a little oil for frying
- a vegetable peeler
- chopping boards, safe knives
- saucepan, colander, masher
- teaspoons, tablespoons, forks
- circular pastry cutter
- frying pan

Links with the Early Learning Goals

PSED work as part of a group or class, taking turns and sharing fairly;
KUW look closely at similarities, differences, patterns & change;
PD use a range of small and large equipment;
CD explore colour, texture, shape, form and space in two and three dimensions.

What you do:

1. Look at the potatoes carefully, their shape, colour, texture, size, eyes and markings.
   The children can work independently most of the time, but it is important to remind them of the dangers of the cooker, hot pans and hot water.
2. Heat the oven to 175C/350F/Gas mark 4.
3. Wash the potatoes in cold water.
4. Peel and wash again. Look at the shape of the peel when it has been removed and compare the inside and outside.
5. On chopping boards, help the children cut each potato into small pieces. Spike the potato on a fork to help steady it.
6. Put the pieces in the saucepan and cover with cold water. Add the salt.
7. Put the pan on the cooker and bring to the boil.
8. When the water bubbles turn down the heat and leave the potatoes to cook slowly for about 15 minutes.
9. When soft, drain the potatoes at a sink, using the colander.
10. Put the potatoes back in the saucepan. Add the milk and butter.
11. Let the children take turns at mashing the potatoes until they are soft and fairly smooth.
12. Help them mix in the cheese and leave to cool.
13. Divide into four and shape into rounds using their hands. This can be quite messy and it helps to dust their hands and the mashed potato pile lightly with flour. You can use a cutter to shape the cakes, or leave them 'natural'.
14. Heat the oil in the frying pan, add the cakes and fry until slightly browned on both sides.

And another idea . . .

* Put the mixture into an ovenproof dish and bake for about 15 minutes.
* Leave some potatoes in a dark place to sprout.

Fruit Kebabs

Fruit kebabs are a good way to encourage children to eat more fruit and introduce them to new flavours. As well as familiar fruit try to include one or two exotic fruits, such as mango, papaya or pineapple.

What you need:

- wooden skewers or small plastic straws
- a variety of fruit
- vegetable knife, dessert knife, forks, chopping board
- aprons
- plates and bowls
- plain yogurt
- honey

Links with the Early Learning Goals

PSED be confident to try new activities, initiate ideas & speak in a familiar group;

KUW select the tools and techniques they need to shape, assemble & join the materials they are using;

PD handle tools, objects, construction & malleable materials safely and with increasing control.

What you do:

1. If possible, take the children with you to buy the fruit from a greengrocer or a supermarket.
2. Look at all the fruit before you start. Make sure the children know the names of all the fruit they are about to eat, and use describing words for the smell, feel and look of each. Look at markings and stalks.
3. Wash and peel the fruit thoroughly.
4. Most children will be able to manage to peel a banana but may need assistance with other fruits.
5. Younger children will be able to chop soft fruit, such as banana or kiwi, with a dessert knife.
6. Children using sharper knives will find it easier and safer to hold the fruit in place on the chopping board with a fork.
7. Cut all the fruit into chunks.
8. Put the fruit chunks into a big bowl or smaller separate bowls.
9. Now the children can make their own individual fruit kebabs by threading chunks of fruit onto their own skewer or straw one by one.
10. Mix the yogurt with some honey for a dipping sauce.

And another idea . . .

* Plant some of the seeds from the fruit to see which will grow.
* Read **Handa's Surprise** by Eileen Browne and use the fruit mentioned in the story.
* For a real treat try dipping strawberries into plain yogurt (or even melted chocolate!).

Pile it High

Make this colourful sweet with any seasonal fruit (or even your school fruit from the Healthy Schools Scheme).

What you need:
- a selection of chopped fruit, such as strawberries, other berries, bananas, grapes, kiwi
- crème fraiche or yogurt
- small soft sweets to decorate
- teaspoons
- plastic cups – preferably transparent

Links with the Early Learning Goals

PSED select and use activities and resources independently;
MD talk about, recognise & recreate simple patterns;
PD recognise the importance of keeping healthy and those things which contribute to this;
CLL extend their vocabulary, exploring the meanings & sounds of new words.

What you do:

1. Look at the ingredients together and ask the children to choose what they would like to include in their dessert. Talk about eating fruit to keep healthy and that sweets are a treat.
2. Help the children to chop up the bigger fruits and put each fruit in a separate bowl. Make bowls of the smaller fruit and berries.
3. Each child can now take a cup and put some of the chopped fruit in the bottom of the cup with a teaspoon (good hand control practice!).
4. Add a layer of crème fraiche or yogurt.
5. Continue layering fruit and crème fraiche or yogurt.
6. Finish with a layer of crème fraiche/yogurt.
7. Look the pattern of the layers of fruit and cream.
8. Decorate with just a few sweets.
9. Enjoy your Knickerbocker Glories together! If the sun is shining take them outside.

And another idea . . .

* Mix paints to recreate the colours of the fruit used; for example, bright green and black for the inside of a kiwi. Paint a picture.
* Collect pictures of fruit from magazines or recipe cards (free from supermarkets) for a collage.
* Set up an ice cream parlour in the role play area
* Take some photos of fruit at a greengrocers or market. Make an album.

Banana Custard

Most children like bananas, but other soft fruits work too. This is a recipe for baked custard, which will introduce children to using a water bath or Bain Marie. You could use tinned or packet custard instead.

What you need for a group of children:
- 2 bananas
- 4 teaspoons of jam
- 2 eggs
- a pint of milk
- a little butter or margarine
- shallow ovenproof dish
- larger dish or roasting tin
- balloon whisk
- mixing bowl
- dessert knives
- chopping board

Links with the Early Learning Goals

CLL extend their vocabulary, exploring the meanings & sounds of new words;
KUW ask questions about why things happen and how things work;
PD handle tools, objects, construction & malleable materials safely and with increasing control;
use a range of small and large equipment.

The Little Book of Cooking Together

What you do:

1. Look at this recipe with the children, check the ingredients and equipment you need, and make sure they know the names of everything you will use.
2. Talk about how a water bath works, by heating up water in the outside container to cook the custard without boiling it.
3. Heat the oven 200°C/400°F/Gas mark 6. The children can do the next stages.
4. Rub the butter over the inside of the smaller dish.
5. Peel and slice the bananas using the dessert knife and chopping board.
6. Cover the bottom of the dish with the sliced banana.
7. Spoon the jam on top of the bananas.
8. Using a whisk, mix the sugar, egg and milk together in the mixing bowl and pour over the bananas and jam
9. Place the large dish on the oven shelf, pour in water until the container is one-quarter full, then place the smaller dish containing the banana mixture into the larger dish.
10. Bake in the oven for approximately 25 minutes.
11. Remove from the oven and look at what has happened to the custard.
12. Eat the custard while it is still warm, but not too hot!

And another idea . . .

* Show the children how to peel a banana by holding the stalk, which will give them a 'handle' to hold while eating it.
* Talk about the different shades of the yellow in the banana, its skin and the custard, and set up a colour table with a focus on yellow.

Toss a Pancake

Pancakes can be served as a savoury or sweet dish. They are good to make for Shrove Tuesday, which is the day before Lent starts and takes place during February or March.

What you need:
- 125g self-raising flour
- 1 egg
- 300ml milk
- 1 tablespoon sunflower oil, plus more for frying
- scales
- measuring jug
- tablespoons, teaspoons
- mixing bowls
- whisk, sieve, fork
- frying pan, spatula
- lemon juice, sugar, jam or cheese for fillings

Links with the Early Learning Goals

MD use language such as 'circle' or 'bigger' to describe the shape and size of solids & flat shapes;

CD explore colour, texture, shape, form & space in 2 & 3 dimensions;

PD move with control and coordination.

The Little Book of Cooking Together

What you do:

1. The children can work independently for most of this activity, but they need a warning not to get close to the cooker and hot pans, and of course, an adult will be doing the cooking!
2. Talk about the ingredients, read the recipe together and let the children collect the things you need. Check that they know the names of all the utensils.
3. Now the children can break the eggs into the measuring jug and add the milk and oil, mixing them together well.
4. Help the children to sieve the flour into the mixing bowl. Make a small hollow in the middle of the flour and pour the egg mixture in a bit at a time, whisking all the time.
5. Let the children take turns to whisk the mixture thoroughly until smooth. Putting a folded cloth under the bowl will help to steady it.
6. Heat a little oil in the frying pan and add 3 spoonfuls of pancake mixture.
7. Tilt the pan to spread the mixture and cook until the pancake has formed.
8. Flip over to cook the other side.
9. Offer lemon and sugar, jam, chocolate spread or cheese to fill the pancakes.

And another idea . . .

* Use a citrus press to squeeze fresh lemons.
* Read the story The Enormous Pancake.
* Sing:
  'Mix a pancake, stir a pancake,
  Pop it in the pan;
  Fry a pancake, toss a pancake,
  Catch it if you can.'

Baked Apples

Try this recipe in the autumn, when apples are cheap (or even free from a generous parent). Smaller, eating apples may be more manageable to prepare and sweeter to eat than huge cooking apples.

What you need:
- 4 cooking apples
- 60g caster sugar or a spoonful of honey for each apple (sweeter apples may need less or even no sweetening)
- mixed dried fruit (packet)
- apple corer, fork
- teaspoons, chopping board
- large ovenproof dish or deep baking tray (no metal in microwaves!)
- oven gloves
- conventional or microwave oven

Links with the Early Learning Goals

CLL extend their vocabulary, exploring the meanings & sounds of new words;

KUW investigate objects & materials by using all of their senses; ask questions about why things happen and how things work;

CD explore colour, texture, shape, form & space in two & three dimensions.

What you do:

1. Take time to look closely at the apples, their similarities and differences. Look at shape, size, colour and texture of skin. Talk about what an apple is (it's a fruit with seeds inside) and how the apple gives the seeds moisture and protection as they grow. Remind children that the seeds in apples that fall on the ground and don't get eaten may grow into new apple trees.
2. Now talk about the recipe, the ingredients and what you are going to do. Look at the apple corer and talk about how it works.
3. Get the children to wash the apples thoroughly.
4. Core the apples together. Make sure the children use the corer <u>down</u> through the apple onto a board or a folded teatowel. Pierce the skin with a fork in several places (this stops the skin splitting) and put the apples in the baking dish or tray.
5. Look at the cores and collect some seeds to grow.
6. Mix the dried fruit and sugar together.
7. Fill the centre of each apple with the dried fruit mixture, adding a teaspoonful at a time.
8. Pour about 1cm. of water in the baking dish or tray to stop the apples burning on the bottom.
9. Bake in the middle of the oven for 35 to 40 minutes, until tender, or in a microwave for 7-9 minutes on High.
10. Make sure the apples cool before eating, they get VERY hot in the middle! Eat by themselves or with custard or cream.

And another idea . . .

* Taste a variety of apples, and compare flavours – especially the sourness of cooking apples.
* Plant some of the apple pips and watch them sprout.

Choc Chip Muffins

This recipe makes 12 muffins. You can make muffins in a microwave too, so this is a good recipe for those of you without a conventional oven in your setting.

What you need for 12 muffins:
- 50g margarine or butter
- 150g of self-raising flour
- 50g of caster sugar
- 1/2 teaspoon baking powder
- 1 egg
- 110 ml of milk
- 120g chocolate chips
- saucepan, sieves, scales
- small and large mixing bowls
- teaspoons, wooden spoons, forks
- measuring jug
- muffin tins or paper cases
- skewer, oven gloves

Links with the Early Learning Goals

PSED work as part of a group or class;
CLL interact with others, negotiating plans and activities and taking turns in conversation;
MD say and use number names in order in familiar contexts;
PD handle tools, objects, construction & malleable materials safely and with increasing control.

The Little Book of Cooking Together

What you do:

1. Chocolate chip muffins are a favourite with many children and they will all enjoy learning how to make them. You could make picture cards of the recipe with a stage on each card (use a digital camera for the pictures). Then the children can follow the recipe in sequence, noticing the changes as each ingredient is added, melted or mixed.
2. Heat the oven to 200C/400F/Gas 6.
3. Melt the margarine in the saucepan over a low heat or in the microwave for a few seconds.
4. Work with the children on the rest of the recipe.
5. Sieve the flour into the large mixing bowl.
6. Add the sugar and the baking powder. Mix everything together with the wooden spoon.
7. Break the egg into the small bowl and whisk it with the fork.
8. Add the egg and the milk to the saucepan of melted, cooled margarine and mix well.
9. Pour it into the flour and mix everything together with a fork.
10. Mix in the chocolate chips and divide the mixture into paper cases or tins. Use the spatula to scrape out the bowl.
11. Put the muffins in the oven for 20 minutes or the microwave for 3 minutes on full power. When cooked, the muffins should be golden and risen. Check by pushing a skewer into the middle of one muffin. If it comes out clean the muffins are cooked. If not cook for a bit longer.
12. Leave to cool before eating.

And another idea . . .
* Replace the chocolate chips with 2 peeled and chopped bananas.
* Make several batches to sell at fund raising events.
* Offer plain play dough and paper cases for play.

Make a Teddy Face

Most children will be able to make a teddy face without too much difficulty, but the recipe can be made simpler if you wish, by omitting the last three steps, just making the face with choc chips.

What you need for 4 children:
- 180g margarine or butter
- 115g sugar
- 225g self raising flour
- flour for surface
- 1 tablespoon jam
- choc chips or raisins for eyes
- weighing scales
- mixing bowl
- wooden spoon, tablespoon
- medium sized round cutter
- greased baking tray
- cooling rack
- a teddy bear for a model

Links with the Early Learning Goals

MD say and use number names in order in familiar contexts in practical activities & discussion begin to use the vocabulary involved in adding & subtracting;

CD explore colour, texture, shape, form & space in 2 & 3 dimensions;

PD handle tools, objects, construction & malleable materials safely and with increasing control.

What you do:

1. Talk together about the recipe and the ingredients. Think about what a teddy looks like (you could bring one to the group as a model).
2. **Heat the oven to 180°C/350°F/Gas mark 5.** The children can do all the rest till point 11 with minimal help from you.
3. Measure the margarine and sugar into the bowl and use the tablespoon to mix them together until creamy.
4. Stir the jam into the mixture.
5. Add the flour, 2 tablespoons at a time. Get the children to count at every opportunity!
6. Sprinkle a little flour on a board or clean work surface and flatten the mixture to approximately 1cm thick.
7. Cut out a circle using the cutter and place on a baking tray.
8. Look at the shape of the bear's ears.
9. Now roll some of the mixture to the size and shape of a marble, break it in half and press the pieces in the right places on the biscuit to make ears.
10. Use chocolate chips or raisins for eyes and mouth to complete the face.
11. Put on a baking tray and **cook for approximately 18 minutes until golden brown. Lift carefully onto a wire tray and cool before eating.**

And another idea . . .

* Dance to The Teddy Bear's Picnic music.
* Have a Teddy Bears' Picnic
* Tell Bear stories:
  Goldilocks and The 3 Bears
  It's The Bear!
  Where's My Teddy!
  This is the Bear
  Bears in the Night
  Peace at Last
  and others!

The Little Book of Cooking Together

Jam Tarts

This must be the favourite children's recipe of all time! You can fill the tarts with fruit puree or sugar free pie filling for a healthier option, or make savoury tarts with a tomato sauce filling.

What you need:

- 150g plain flour
- 75g margarine
- 12 teaspoons cold water
- pinch of salt
- strawberry jam or other filling
- mixing bowl
- tablespoon
- small rolling pins
- greased tart tray tin
- round cutters to fit your tins
- oven gloves
- cooling rack

Links with the Early Learning Goals

CD explore colour, texture, shape, form & space in 2&3 dimensions;
KUW look closely at similarities, differences, patterns & change; ask questions about why things happen and how things work;
PD handle tools, objects, construction & malleable materials safely and with increasing control.

What you do:
1. Heat the oven to 200°C/400°F/gas mark 6.
2. This is a very easy recipe for children to do with little help from you. Your role will be to talk, help, question and support them in being as independent as possible.
3. Help the children to measure the flour and salt into the mixing bowl.
4. Show them how to use their fingers to rub in the margarine so that it looks like crumbs. Observe together how the mixture changes as ingredients are combined.
5. Add the water (counting the spoonfuls as you put them in) and mix in using the tablespoon.
6. Now, using their hands, squeeze the mixture into a ball.
7. Next, they need to sprinkle flour on the work surface, share the pastry between the members of the group and roll it out thinly using the small rolling pins.
8. Cut the pastry into shapes using the round cutters.
9. Put the shapes into the greased tart tin and fill with a teaspoon of jam or other filling of their choice.
10. Bake the tarts for about 15 minutes
11. Remove from the tin and leave to cool on a rack before eating (the jam will be very hot).

And another idea . . .
* Add some grated cheese with the margarine for a savoury pastry.
* Play the nursery rhyme The Queen of Hearts.
* Add rolling pins, tins and cutters to play dough so the children can keep practicing the skills of rolling, cutting etc.

Banana Fudge For Divali

Make this fudge at Divali time, it is an Asian favourite. It needs quite a lot of adult support and some steps are 'adult only'. It also suits people with a very sweet tooth, so once a year may do!

What you need:
- 1 banana
- 2 cardamom pods
- 25g margarine
- 50g semolina
- 50g ground almonds
- 50g brown sugar
- 4 tablespoons water
- hot plate or cooker
- bowl, forks, tablespoons
- mortar & pestle or rolling pin
- saucepan, wooden spoons
- scales, shallow tin
- greaseproof paper

Links with the Early Learning Goals

PSED have a developing respect for their own cultures and beliefs and those of other people;

KUW begin to know about cultures and beliefs of others;

PD handle tools, objects, construction & malleable materials safely and with increasing control.

The Little Book of Cooking Together

What you do:
1. Look closely at the cardamom pods together and talk about the shape and texture. Cut open a pod, look at the seeds and talk about the smell. Pour a little semolina out to for children to feel with their fingers. Talk about the recipe.
2. Let the children peel the banana, break it into small pieces into the bowl and mash with a fork.
3. Remove the cardamom seeds from the pods and crush in a mortar and pestle (or in a plastic bag with a rolling pin) and add to the banana.
4. Melt the margarine in the saucepan.
5. Add the semolina and cook gently for 2 minutes.
6. Remove from the heat and cool.
7. Stir in the banana mix, ground almonds, sugar and water. Mix thoroughly.
8. Return to the heat and bring to the boil.
9. Stir continuously until the mixture thickens and comes away from the sides of the pan.
10. Grease the tin and pour the mixture into the tin.
11. Leave in the fridge to set for about 2 hours. Compare the fudge before and after chilling.
12. Cut into small squares.
    Allow the children to work independently as much as possible, but it is important that the children do not get close to the cooker or pan while it is hot.

And another idea . . .
* Wrap the fudge and let the children take it home as a special gift.
* Read the story of Rama and Sita.
* For a banana 'lollipop' peel bananas, wrap in cling film and freeze.

Hot Chocolate

Making hot chocolate in the winter time provides an opportunity to talk about the changes in season and keeping warm when it's cold outside. It's great after a walk!

What you need:
- drinking chocolate powder
- milk
- teaspoons
- beakers
- saucepan
- hot ring or microwave

Links with the Early Learning Goals

PSED have a developing awareness of their own needs, views & feelings and be sensitive to the needs, views and feelings of others;

KUW begin to know about cultures and beliefs of others; investigate objects & materials using all of their senses.

What you do:
1. Let the children measure two teaspoons of chocolate powder into their own beaker.
2. Then they can add enough milk so that the chocolate can be stirred to a thick paste.
3. Heat the milk gently in the saucepan or a microwave and make sure it is a safe temperature before giving to the children.
4. Pour some milk into each child's beaker and mix until it is dissolved into the chocolate.
5. You could sprinkle some grated chocolate or chocolate powder on the top before drinking, or for a special treat, dip a chocolate flake in!

And another idea . . .
* Add small pieces of solid chocolate instead of the drinking chocolate and observe the difference.
* Try making iced chocolate or chocolate milkshake by cooling the chocolate milk and foaming it in a blender or adding ice cubes.
* Put a cup of hot chocolate outside and one in a warm room. Check at intervals to see which cools first.
* Set up a discovery table and collect items that keep us warm, eg hats, scarves, gloves, hot water bottle, quilt.

Milk Shakes & Smoothies

Making milk shakes and smoothies is a delicious way of meeting the Five Fruits and Vegetables a Day target. It is also a very good way to use up over ripe fruit.

What you need:
- 1 pint milk
- approximately 320g soft fruit such as banana, strawberry or kiwi (berries are really good for this recipe)
- small knife
- hand held electric blender,
- rotary or balloon whisk
- dessert knife and fork
- chopping board
- large bowl
- measuring jug
- beakers, straws

Links with the Early Learning Goals

PSED be confident to try new activities, initiate ideas & speak in a familiar group;

KUW find out about & identify the uses of everyday technology;

PD handle tools, objects, construction & malleable materials safely; recognise the importance of keeping healthy and those things which contribute to this.

What you do:

1. Look closely at and feel each fruit. Talk together about how bananas change when they are mashed and milk is added.
2. Look at the equipment you need. Talk about how each piece works. If you are using a rotary or balloon whisk, let the children have a turn and watch the way it works.
3. Help the children to wash the fruit thoroughly and peel it if necessary.
4. Place the fruit in a bowl and mash it down using a fork. Watch the changes in colour and texture as the fruit is squished and mixed.
5. Add the milk and place the blender into the bowl. Ensure that it is touching the bottom and remains there while blending. Switch on and blend the mixture until smooth. Alternatively you could use a rotary or balloon whisk, then the children could do the mixing themselves.
6. Help the children to pour the shakes into individual beakers and add a straw.

And another idea . . .

* Replace some of the milk with natural yogurt for a creamier shake.
* Pour the mixture into lolly moulds and freeze.
* Do a milkshake dance, encouraging the children to use their whole bodies. Try bendy bananas jumping in the bowl, or blenders whizzing round and round, add sounds to match.
* For further information about 5 A Day: www.dh.gov.uk/healthtopics

Fruit Punch

You can combine almost any kind of fruit juices to make fruit punch. This recipe uses fresh fruit so the children can learn where juices come from

What you need:
- 2 oranges
- 1 diced mango (or other soft fruit)
- 1 fresh, or a small can of pineapple
- 100ml water
- 4 mint leaves
- 1 lemon
- vegetable knives
- chopping boards
- citrus squeezer
- large bowl
- ladle, beakers, straws

Links with the Early Learning Goals

CLL extend their vocabulary, exploring the meanings & sounds of new words;

KUW investigate objects & materials by using all of their senses; find out about and identify the uses of everyday technology;

PD handle tools, objects, construction & malleable materials safely and with increasing control.

What you do:
1. Involve the children in describing the fruit before and after it is peeled, and introduce new words such as spiky, blend and pulp. Talk about the smell and texture of both peel and flesh. At each stage discuss how the fruit has changed. Read the recipe together.
2. Examine the oranges and cut them in half.
3. Using a citrus squeezer, extract the juice from the oranges and add to the bowl.
4. Peel and dice the mango, pineapple and any other soft fruit.
5. Put the fruit into a bowl and place the blender into the bowl. Ensure that it is touching the bottom and remains there while blending. Switch on and blend the mixture until smooth.
6. Pour the water into the bowl and stir gently.
7. Wash the lemon thoroughly and let the children examine it.
8. Using a vegetable knife, cut the lemon into slices and add to the bowl. Wash the mint leaves and add to the punch.
9. Look at how the mint and lemon are floating.
10. Ladle the punch into individual beakers and add a straw to each. This is a great treat for drinking in the garden on a summer day.

And another idea . . .
* Give each child a mint leaf and let them rub it to release the smell.
* Use sparkling water to make fizzy punch.
* Add cinnamon and cloves to the punch and heat gently to make a festive drink for Christmas or a winter day.

Tea Tasters' Time

This may seem a strange thing to include in a cookery book, but drinking tea has been part of our culture for hundreds of years. This activity provides lots of scope for experiment and discussion.

What you need:
- teas – leaf and bag, including some herb and fruit teas
- milk
- sugar
- kettle and water
- teapots or jugs
- milk jug
- tea strainer
- teaspoons
- cups or beakers

Links with the Early Learning Goals

PSED be confident to try new activities, initiate ideas & speak in a familiar group;
KUW investigate objects & materials by using all of their senses; ask questions about why things happen and how things work;
PD handle tools, objects, construction & malleable materials safely and with increasing control.

What you do:

1. There is a good selection of teas in all supermarkets, as well as speciality shops. Aim for a balance of strong and mild flavours. Look for Lapsang Souchong, a black tea from China or Earl Grey, which has a perfumed aroma and flavour.
   Indian teas vary too; Assam has a rich flavour and Darjeeling has a delicate flavour and aroma.
   Fruit teas are usually sweet and have a milder flavour, but still give off a strong fruit fragrance.
   Include herb teas, such as peppermint or camomile. Although it is essential that an adult pours the boiling water the children can mostly work independently.
2. Examine the leaf tea first. Touch, smell and compare the differences between the types.
3. Cut open one or two tea bags and compare with the loose tea. Open some fruit tea bags and see what is in them.
4. Ask each child to put one teaspoon of tea leaves (or one bag) into a teapot, mug or heatproof jug. Count as you go.
5. Warn the children about the hot water as you pour it onto the tea.
6. Tell the children that you all need to wait for a few minutes while the tea 'brews' and flavours 'infuse'.
7. Sing 'Polly Put the Kettle On' while you wait. Change the names of Susie and Suki to the names of the children making the tea.
8. Repeat the process with some other tea varieties.
9. Talk about the smell and colour of each tea.
10. Pour the tea into individual cups or beakers, using a strainer for the leaf tea.
11. Add milk. Encourage the children to try the tea without sugar.
12. Add a little sugar for children who want it.
13. Examine and talk about the wet tea leaves and tea bags together.

And another idea . . .
* Set up a discovery table with items such as teapots, tea cosies, tins and caddies, spoons, and strainers and all the different teas.

Try the Tea Council website (www.teatrail.co.uk) for stories, games & puzzles.

If you have found this book useful you might also like ...

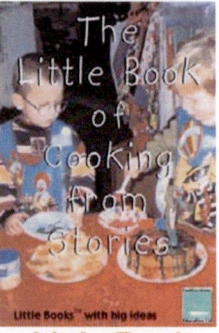

The Little Book of Cooking From Stories
LB7
ISBN 1-904187-04-8

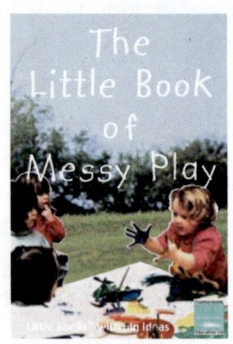

The Little Book of Messy Play
LB13
ISBN 1-904187-09-9

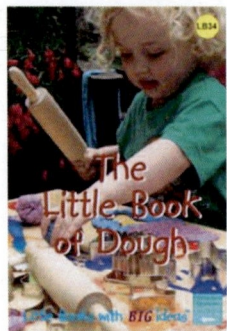

The Little Book of Dough
LB36
ISBN 1-905019-10-6

The Little Book of Investigations
LB20
ISBN 1-904187-66-8

All available from

Featherstone Education   PO Box 6350
Lutterworth   LE17 6ZA
T:0185 888 1212   F:0185 888 1360

on our web site
www.featherstone.uk.com

and from selected
book suppliers